The Lemons of Life

The Lemons of Life

"Squeezing the most out of Life's Lemons"

ISMAEL LARA

Copyright © 2021 by Ismael Lara.

ISBN: 978-1-956230-00-0

All rights reserved. No part of this book may be reproduced or transmitted in any form or by any means, electronic or mechanical, including photocopying, recording, or by any information storage and retrieval system, without permission in writing from the copyright owner.

CONTENTS

Introduction..7
Life is a Garden..11
Lemons in the Limelight..16
Demystifying Life's lemons...17
Lemons Are Not All That We Get...18
Lemons Are Only Temporary..22
Lemons must be kept in Perspective...24
Lemons might be your Opportunity..28
A Proactive Approach to Life's Lemons...................................34
Balancing Your Lemons..43
Responses to Life's Lemons..49
The Lemon's Product Enterprise System..................................57
The Anatomy of Lemons...63
Conclusion...68

Introduction

It's no secret that every single one of us, as long as we are alive, at one point or another, will experience difficult times in our lives. While the situations may vary in intensity, we will all be faced with challenges that shake our sense of stability and comfort. There's an age-old saying commonly used in the face of obstacles that states, "when life gives you lemons, make some lemonade". It is the characteristics of lemons that bring forth this metaphor of life. When life gives us challenges and hard times, they will be sour in comparison with the other sweet and tasty experiences that we expect for life to provide to us. Sometimes the tanginess of life becomes so strong that we begin to focus on the challenge alone and lose sight of everything else. We see "Life" as sour. Needless to say, this is not a productive approach to living. The more that we dwell on the problems in life, the more we will taste the bitterness of our lemons. But here's something interesting, we know that lemons are meant to be sour, but somehow we forget that they are not meant to be consumed alone. Think about it. Lemons are best used in combination with other things like sugar, salt, or chili powder, and they can be used to add a burst of flavor to our meats and vegetables while, at the same time, serving as a flavor enhancer to our waters. You see, there is so much more to your lemons than you may know. I created this book, "The Lemons of Life", to share my experiences with you as well as some things that you can do when life gives YOU lemons. The main goal is to encourage you to fixate on the solutions, rather than the problems. My hope is that you will be able to focus on how you can make lemonade, and maybe even something else, when life brings opposition, or lemons, your way!

In order to set the stage for the book, let me tell you a little bit about me. Not only have I experienced a plethora of lemons in life, but I have also learned to overcome them with time and wisdom. However, not only have I learned to overcome them, but I've also witnessed the power of sharing what I've learned during my process with anybody who is willing to listen and learn. This is part of my story. One significant challenge that I have faced was having to adapt to what is known as a "new normal". Some time ago, as I was serving in the military, I was given a round of immunizations that had an adverse effect on my body. Due to these immunizations, and their subsequent side effects, I lost a considerable amount of muscle and bone mass as well as my ability to digest food properly, exercise, walk long distances, stand for prolonged periods of time, and even my will to live. By taking a wide range of anti-depressants, anti-inflammatories, random medicines, and painkillers, I constantly kept hurting myself and making my situation worse than it already was. After returning to my civilian job as a fourth grade teacher, I found myself unable to serve my students the way that I used to. I was broken and unable to do what I loved most... shape the future one child at a time. It's not that I didn't try. On the contrary, I did! I followed all the advice that people gave me and kept on giving it my 100%. Yet, it wasn't enough. On one occasion, after having been rushed to the emergency room during one of my classes by my principal, I was medically disabled by my neurologist. It was at this point that I had to make a choice. I could push on and keep making a difference or I could simply give up. I wish I could say that I pushed on and I lived happily ever after, but I didn't. I gave up. I resigned from my job and gave up on life. I said farewell to my students believing that their new teacher would be able to serve them better than I and then I just stayed home. I didn't leave. I just locked myself in. For a year it seemed like I was dying slowly. I had never experienced anything so physically and mentally challenging before. I found it so hard to convince or motivate myself to push forward. Not only had I lost my

Introduction

health and sense of self, I lost all hope as well. Once defeat took over, I no longer found it possible to believe. Things just got worse as I struggled to do simple things like change my newborn's diaper, hold him in my arms to feed him, or carry him from his crib to the bed. Marital problems escalated in response to the sudden change in my behavior and abilities. I was terrible company to be around and I was slowly losing my relationships. The bills piled up, became past due, and the foreclosure notice eventually arrived. Everything I had worked so hard for in a lifetime was slipping out of my grasp. It was over. Or at least I thought it was.

In one of the darkest moments of my life, I was forced to face all of my fears and insecurities. I was compelled to accept my past, face my present, re-envision my future and then let go. I released two things that I loved and hold dear to my heart: serving my country and teaching children, in hopes that I would find new ways of living and better means to help others. I counted my losses, made some changes, and decided to return to work. I did so slowly and gradually by buying and selling auctioned surplus items on eBay, Amazon, Offer Up, and Craigslist on my own time. In doing so, I began to improve my physical and emotional well-being and was faring somewhat better. However, my heart would still crave for the need to make a difference in the world through education. I knew I couldn't teach anymore but maybe I could do something else. During that time, I stumbled upon a unique job posting for a program site coordinator at a school. I was terrified to apply but something inside me compelled me to do it. Fast forward a few weeks and I got the job. So, I took the dive! While I wasn't able to teach students firsthand, I decided to teach everyone on my team what I knew. I figured that although I lacked the physical stamina and strength to teach students, I definitely had the means to teach adults how to better serve their students in creative classroom settings. I implemented the strategy of replication, which I share in detail in my book "Spearhead Leadership" and, with some hard work, was able to pass my knowledge to others rather than giving up on education and serving altogether. I served a total of 250 students and lead a team of 13 people that year. That was 10 times what I was used to in a regular classroom. As of the writing of this book, I am a proud project director for enrichment programs serving over 1200 children and their families annually and overseeing over 75 staff members while training them to be the best educators and future leaders that they can be. I know it isn't much in comparison to what others have accomplished. But for me, it means the world. Even serving one child would be more than enough. And I will always continue to grow. On my spare time, I write children's books, self-help books, provide leadership consulting services, and am in the process of starting a non-profit aimed at providing STEAM activities and resources to children all over the world. The project is called STEAMspirations™. You see, I went from receiving horrible lemons in life to mustering up the courage to take my lemons, vest my lemons, and move forward with my life. It has not been easy and there are tons of people who have it a lot harder, but in the grand scheme of things, life is not as bad as we think. I've seen my brothers and sisters in arms who lost limbs and/or were disfigured still running marathons and participating in a plethora of limitless activities. I've seen impoverished children in third world countries walk for miles just to attend school. I've seen cancer survivors and illness fighters push on and never give up despite the diagnosis. I've seen the poor and marginalized rise to positions of wealth and authority through honest work and perseverance. I decided that if they could make it, I could as well. Even when the going gets tough, life is still not as bad as we believe. In this book, I will share a few concepts that can assist the many individuals who have been experiencing difficulties in turning the lemons of life into meaningful and even rewarding experiences.

Life is a Garden

A powerful metaphor for life can be that of a garden. At birth, we start off with a planter, some soil, and a few plants that our family provided for us. During this time, our experiences are interpreted and buffered by our parents and family since infants do not have the capacity to fully interpret their own experiences. These experiences can be likened to plants, some of which will eventually grow to become fruit-bearing trees. There are trees for learning, trees for enjoyment, trees for many other things, and even some random plants based on our unique experiences. Initially, our families tend to and nurture those plants and they start to grow. However, as we grow physically and cognitively, we begin to interact with the world around us. This creates the foundation for our personal experiences and the development of our persona, perspective, and world view. At this stage, we transplant our existing plants into our very own patch of ground. This "patch" is the basis for the human experience. Every healthy human being will have, at a minimum, the opportunity to experience the world around them at least at this capacity. It is in this stage that the responsibility becomes ours and we are able to tend and nurture the plants that we started with, neglect them, and/or plant other things. This is done so by what we experience and what we allow into our lives. If we tend to our health, then our health tree will be big and strong. But, if we neglect it, through inadequate diet, exercise, and stress we can't be surprised if our tree is dry, brittle, and colorless. A similar process exists for all the other things in our life. As we grow older, we add experiences to our existing trees and even plant new ones altogether. For example, when we start school we plant our formal education tree. We then get to choose how much care, time, and effort we want to invest in it. We can tend it until primary school, high school, university, and/or postgraduate school if we like. Additionally, we have a general education tree that grows with every new piece of knowledge we learn throughout life. Then, there are those plants, shrubs, and trees that we plant ourselves that are not very positive, healthy, and/or productive for us. We do this consciously and unconsciously via our lifestyle and choices. Needless to say, these will inevitably lead to difficulties down the road. For example, let's say that we decide to engage in risky behavior and we plant the seed of "risk" in our garden. The more we engage in the behavior the bigger and stronger the tree will get, right? Eventually, it will seek to reproduce itself and bear its own kind of fruit. It is that fruit, whatever it may be, that is the final result of our investment in it. For risky behavior, the fruit can be running out of luck or facing really, really hard times. For prejudice, the fruit may be "thinking" that you are far superior to everyone else and irrevocably isolating yourself from those different than you. For bad health habits, it can result in chronic illness and disease. I don't mean to sound morbid, but the information is true. We reap what we sow. Yet, that can also be a good thing. You see, most of the time, we get to decide what we plant and what we will nurture. As it is "our" garden, we play a huge role in its state, composition, and upkeep. We have the option to plant good things and nurture beneficial habits. Doing so will provide a healthy, well-kept, and clean garden of life. Yet, somehow there will always be lemons and lemon trees that we nurture. We just can't get around that fact and it would benefit us to know how to identify them in whatever shape or form they may come in.

What came first... the lemon or the lemon tree?

No one knows what came first but I do know that lemon trees may exist in our garden at different stages of development. We can either plant an entire lemon tree, a small lemon plant, or just a seed. This is important because some problems are immediate and quickly identifiable while others are slow to grow and we tend to miss them until they sprout up and surprise us. Knowing this allows for us to know that, *just because things seem fine on the surface of our garden, it doesn't mean that everything is fine underground*. This is particularly important in regard to the seeds that we plant unknowingly. There are certain habits and attitudes that we engage in that don't really affect us immediately. Since we don't see any immediate negative results, we think that it is safe to continue with the practice. It isn't until way later that we find that the small lemon seeds we ignored in the past are now huge problem-producing trees. Here's a tip, always remember that it's way easier to pull out a small plant than to attempt to uproot or chop down an entire tree. Seriously! My hometown is in the desert and it's common to see many tumbleweeds rolling around. But, have you ever had to pull one out when it is fresh and green? It's not easy. One time, I neglected the weeds in my backyard to the extent that I had to use a Skid-Steer to clear them up. It looked like a jungle! In the same way, when we neglect those small weeds in our lives, we can end up with the same problem and in need of heavy help. If we understand this, we can keep a close eye on the results of our actions and respond accordingly. If we see the slightest hint of problematic tendencies then we know we need to closely monitor that habit, behavior, or practice before it gets out of hand. We might even need to discontinue it altogether.

Uninvited Guests

So far, we've discussed our contributions to the state of our garden and the ways that we may allow lemons into our garden. We also know that we have the privilege and ultimate responsibility for what we allow into our lives. But what about the things we don't plant? What about trouble and difficulty that comes out of nowhere? We may ask ourselves, "How is that fair?" The truth is that it's not. Life isn't fair. Circumstances don't play fair. There will always be things that others have done to us or things that life just brings about. We have no control over them and they just end up in our peaceful little garden and cause chaos. Here's why this book is so important. Life isn't fair but it is our interpretation of events, as well as our response to them, that makes all the difference. We can either ignore the tree and let it grow until it eventually ruins our life. Or, we can identify it, look for any opportunities that it may present, and then choose how much attention we will give it. Any tree or plant will eventually dry and shrivel up without attention and nutrients. We have the option of what to do with them. Whether we nurture them or pull them out by the roots, it's all up to us!

Hopefully, this metaphorical analogy helped you better understand the concept of life giving you lemons. It doesn't just randomly drop them off at your doorstep, they grow in your garden! Some we plant while some are planted for us by life. The question then is... why? The answer is that life is always seeking for balance and it can be seen all around us. There will be good times as well as tough times. There will be fruitful seasons and some of scarcity. It doesn't mean that life is ugly or unfair. It's simply proof that we are still alive and able to experience life. And, that's a really good thing! What this means for us is that we do not need to be afraid of difficult times or challenges. Instead, we need to know that they are a natural byproduct of existence. There is night and day, hot and cold, big and small, good and bad, easy and hard, etc. Opposites are all around us. They create the framework for our experiences as these seek for some type of balance. Now, I don't recommend living in fear expecting for something bad to happen or thinking that life is too good to be true right now and that something has to go wrong soon. Of course not! I simply recommend living with awareness. The best way to assimilate this is to know that challenges might come your way and that you can indeed be prepared with a proactive approach for when they do, if they do. I believe in positivity wholeheartedly and speaking/believing good things over your life but I also will not crumble if something happens that is outside of my control. In fact, when you are ready and prepared for anything, you are able to live a much more fulfilling, positive, and stress-free life. If this wasn't so, then why do we have savings accounts, retirement investments, or health benefits? They are investments in the long-term and a sort of preparation. If we do that with wealth and health, why not with life's many challenges? The question then is, what do we do when life plants a lemon tree in our garden and that bright, yellow fruit starts falling off the tree and on our heads? Should it surprise us? Should we give into worry and despair? No way! We need to be prepared and not let it knock us off of our feet. We need to be ready. The first step in preparing for a challenge is acknowledging its existence and knowing what it's made of. So, let's get up close and personal with those lemons and learn how to deal with them.

Lemons in the Limelight

If you know anything about lemons, you know that they are those yellow, tart, and juicy citrus fruits that have the power to add a kick to anything that is generally bland or flavorless. It is interesting to note that while they belong to the citrus family, they are generally not associated with the sweeter fruits that we are used to like oranges, mandarins, or even grapefruits. Unlike their counterparts, lemons were meant to be sour. And... even though sour is good sometimes, sour by itself is nothing but sour and usually leaves a tangy taste and soured expression on your face. It is this that grants lemons their similarities to the problems and challenges of life. When life happens, it can sometimes sour our existence. However, there is so much more to lemons and our problems than what we know. They may seem like insurmountable odds and unpleasant experiences but we need to remember something. It is "We" that get to decide whether we will empower them or limit their growth in our life. The first step in limiting their effects is to "peel away" any preconceived ideas or notions about lemons, problems, and challenges and to just look at them plainly.

Demystifying Life's lemons

Let's face it. Nobody likes problems, challenges, and/or hard times, especially not really tough ones. That's because these types of trials can throw us off balance and can even be downright intimidating. At first glance, the lemons of life can seem big and scary but with a proper perspective we can learn to see them for what they are and not for what they seem to be. If we remove the fear and mysticism from the naturally occurring process of life's problems, we can truly begin to take control over their effect on our demeanor and attitude when facing them. A really useful strategy when dealing with challenges is to always remember the four premises for demystifying life's lemons.

The Four Premises

1. Lemons are not all that we get
2. Lemons are only temporary
3. Lemons must be kept in perspective
4. Lemons might be your opportunity

By analyzing your challenge using the lenses of these premises you will be able to understand their true nature as well as their potential impact on your life. I believe that this can make a remarkable difference in your response to and success with life's lemons.

Lemons Are Not All That We Get

Would you ever take a bite into a lemon, peel and all? Yuck, right? Well, focusing solely on our problems can have the same effect. We need to be able to see beyond the current challenges and see what else is available to us. You see, **lemons are meant to be sour and bitter, but they are not meant to be consumed alone.** You may feel like you have been on a constant losing streak and that you have piles and piles of lemons. Well, consider this. Life has not only provided lemons to you. Life has given you so much more. Take a good look around you. Have good things happened to you? Have you experienced any wins and breakthroughs? Is there anything good in your life right now? In whatever capacity, I am sure that the answer is yes. We all receive more than just the lemons of life. Remember, life will provide a variety of experiences with the purpose of providing balance and meaningful opportunities to enjoy and appreciate living. You see, lemons are meant to be flavor enhancers in our lives that cause our worlds to be shaken up to the point that we have no other choice than to appreciate and be grateful for the good times and the good things that happen to and for us. Also, lemons allow us to bring out the best in ourselves and they show us what we are capable of. The key is to see things as a whole. Think about it. Maybe life has been decent in providing you with sugar and water. So, when life throws lemons into the equation, you have a few options. You can either drink some water, have a spoonful of sugar by itself, and/or experience the bitterness of the lemons alone. However, you still have other options. Imagine if you mixed the water, sugar, and lemons together, made lemonade, and then enjoyed it. The sourness of the lemons would not taste so bad among your other experiences, right? Then why do we think that we have to eat them alone? It's really because of our tendency to focus on what we don't have or what we need rather than on what we do have available at the moment. Furthermore, everyone will have varying levels of good things present in their lives. So consider this, what if life has been very good to you and you have some steak, chicken, and fish laying around? Huge blessings. Maybe you've received large amounts of money, have a great personality, and/or are skilled or gifted in a craft. How would you view your lemons then? Would you still take them as they are and bite into them? Of course not! You would use the lemons and other spices that life has given you to marinate your meat and enhance their flavors through appreciation. This is truly enlightening! **Lemons directly provide an opportunity for us to appreciate what we have**. They also serve as flavor enhancers for the good things in life. Enhance how? Well, you could pair the lemons of life with what you already have like life, love, friends, health, and ability. If you do this, you'll soon find yourself using those lemons in great meals and new recipes rather than experiencing them on their own. The key to life is to view your situation in its entirety. Don't focus on your lemons. Instead, focus on the bigger picture and you will be surprised at the ultimate amount of uses that your lemons can provide to you. Always remember that we are all birthed into this world with nothing and everything we do have is a combination of what we receive, take, give, earn, and experience. This includes material and immaterial things like memories, triumphs, losses, good breaks, setbacks, etc. Life offers us the full experience. The hard things help us appreciate the good things. If you've never experienced pain, you can never truly appreciate its absence. The same can be said for happiness. If someone has never experienced sadness, there is no way that they would be able to identify and truly appreciate happiness in its fullness. After facing my specific health situation, I was forced on a strict diet and lifestyle for eight years. When I ate certain foods that were not a part of my plan, I felt terribly ill. That was a tough lemon to receive. Imagine not being able to eat all of the goodies that make eating so exciting? Furthermore, imagine losing out on the unique experience of having lunch or dinner with a colleague, family member, or significant other? Well, that was me! When I went to restaurants with others, I was the awkward person in the corner that couldn't eat anything on the menu. Yet, I had to make a choice to change my focus from what I couldn't do to what I could. This was crucial because, for a while, I would dread going to restaurants or even celebrations. I was embarrassed, ashamed, anxious. Instead, I decided to focus on the opportunity to meet with people, network, spend time with them instead of what I was going to eat. My priorities had to change and so did my experience. My breakfast, lunch, and dinner engagements became more meaningful and fulfilling since I started to focus more on people rather than on what I would eat or choose from the menu. Even better, I never argued about where we should go to eat ever again. That was a bonus! So, what would I eat? Well, you might have guessed it. I would eat before or after and in some cases, I would bring my own lunch. Speaking of that, I also decided to focus on the delicious variety of things that I could eat instead of complaining about the things that I couldn't eat. This allowed for me to appreciate and savor every bite, every conversation, and every meeting.

The truth is that we need lemons from time to time. In fact, sometimes we need entire lemon trees. This is the only way that we are able to learn, grow, and become appreciative of the blessings and good things that we receive in life. However, we must be cautious and aware because there is a self-destructive nature that is embedded in many of us that causes us to self-sabotage and engage in things that we are not supposed to involve ourselves in. Some of us subconsciously, or intentionally, like to aggravate the trees that are not good for us. We feel compelled to ruin great things once we achieve them because we feel as if we are unworthy of the progress and success that come with conquering our lemons. We start to shake the lemon tree because we feel like we need more lemons, or hardships to bring us down, to avoid losing our sense of humility. This is not true and is only a figment of our imaginations. By doing this, we often cause certain things to happen to us. If you shake the lemon tree, lemons will fall. More than likely on your head! If you nurture the lemon tree, the tree will produce more lemons and you will inevitably endure long-term issues. Shake the lemon tree if you dare, but do not be surprised when life gives you lemons in return. Instead, respect the lemons and see them as opportunities to grow and learn to appreciate what you do have. Find a balance. Do this and you'll see how the flavor of life may become more enjoyable and satisfying.

Lemons Are Only Temporary

If you've ever had any lemons, then you know that lemons stay fresh for about two weeks when kept out at room temperature. After those two weeks, lemons will essentially dry out and shrivel up. The lemons then become practically useless, are thrown out, and forgotten about. However, did you know that lemons can last up to six weeks in a refrigerator? It's true! You know what else? They can last even longer in the freezer. Three to four months at time! Regardless of the lifespan, it is important to remember that, with time, all things must come to an end. This is one of the most important things to consider because... **lemons are only temporary**. Life is not one giant lemon. Life gives you lemons! Furthermore, lemons were not meant to last forever. If you continue to focus on your lemons in the present you essentially begin conserving them, nurturing them, and extending their lifespan. You must be careful with the way that you view lemons because it is you who gets to make the final decision regarding the shelf life of the lemons in your life. We have all endured some hard times in our lives. The fact that we are still alive and breathing bears witness to the fact that those lemons were only temporary and that we survived the bitterness that came along with experiencing them.

In my journey, I have come to realize that although life is not a lemon, some people actually want it to be a lemon. For some people, it seems easier to blame the lemons for the problems rather than stepping up to the plate and figuring out how to use those lemons for their advantage. For a while, that's what I did! I blamed all my lemons and wouldn't let them go. It was the coping mechanism that I used to be able to get through life. Born illicitly, in high poverty, and a minority. A high school dropout, panhandling on street corners in a third world country, and a stereotypical junkie. You see, it is easier for some individuals to keep the lemons for as long as they can, as a type of crutch, rather than addressing the lemons and doing something about it. Trust me, I get it. I know that life can be extremely difficult at times but difficult times do not last forever. We must learn to let go of the attachment that we have to our lemons so that we can all enjoy the fullness of life and the beauty that life has to offer. Remember that your lemons were not meant to stay fresh forever. Let your lemons dry out and shrivel up! Do not allow the lemons of life to become an excuse for your inability to experience this amazing thing called life. So, the next time you are handed a lemon by life, keep in mind that it is not the first challenge that you have endured and it will not be the last challenge that you will overcome. Always know that your challenges are temporary, you will survive, and it will pass in due time. Stay strong, let go, and move on!

Lemons must be kept in Perspective

Have you ever seen a small building from far away only to find out that it's enormous when you stand in front of it? What about ordering something online only to find out that it's way smaller than it looked in the photo? Well, that's exactly how some of our life experiences can be. There are things in life that are either larger than they look or actually smaller than they seem. The key to all of this is proper perspective. Perspective is the way that we view the world, those around us, and more specifically, our life experiences. Problems and challenges (lemons) will make up some of those experiences. Why is this important? Well, when we face a challenge or obstacle, our current perspective automatically generates a unique perception of it. It is unique to us and is directly related to the way that we view the world. This is important because our response, if any, to the challenge is directly linked to how we perceive it. For some people, a challenge can look like a small stone in their path, while for others, that same challenge can seem like a huge mountain. Same challenge. Different perception. Different response. You see, when lemons show up in your life, they can seem like insurmountable odds or unconquerable challenges. They can seem like massive mountains. Yet, they might not really be as big and menacing as we make them out to be. From personal experience, I can tell you that having the right perspective isn't easy. Yet, I can also tell you that adjusting and even changing your perspective is possible, albeit difficult. When a lemon arrives, it does its best to get your attention and crowd your perspective. Problems are often like that. They crave your attention and want to be in the limelight... No pun intended!

However, we do have a choice on how much we focus on them and how we focus on them. You see, when we hold the lemons in front of our eyes, all that we'll be able to see will be the lemon or lemons. Our entire vision and view is taken over by the challenge or problem. It's difficult to see anything else and we feel like the lemon is all that there is. It's so big that we can't see anything else. However, when you stop focusing on it and pull it away from your face, it starts to look smaller and you're able to see other things around you and in front of you. For example, you're able to see your strong and skilled hands and strong arms. You see capability and capacity. You are capable. Yet, that's still all that you see. The entire background is still out of focus. It's just you and your lemon or lemons. Your skills and abilities versus the problem or challenge. You see yourself alone in your own struggle. This is where most people choose to stay. They deal or try to deal with the issue on their own, struggle, and eventually move on. Sometimes they conquer the lemon and sometimes they just set it aside for later. Yet, there's another way. If you just placed your lemon or lemons on the floor and took several steps back, you would be able to see something entirely different. You would finally see the entire picture unhindered by the depth of field limitation of your vision. You would see a small lemon against the backdrop of all of your life experiences, skills, abilities, and accomplishments. You would be able to see all of the good things that have happened for you and the supportive network of individuals around you like your family and friends. With that, you'd definitely be able to address the problem or take on the challenge more effectively.

Yet, that's not all! What if you took more steps back? What if you stepped completely out of your garden? What would you see then? Well, if you went out far enough, you would see several things. You would be able to see other people's gardens. You would be able to see their own lemons and how they respond to them. You would have a new perspective, right? More open. Your view of life and challenges would be expanded and you would be able to see things for what they really are. And, in doing so, you'd be able to come to the realization that:

1. You're not the only one facing a challenge.
2. You're not the only one facing your current challenge.
3. You're not the only one that has faced your challenge.
4. Your challenge might not be as difficult as those of others.

When we realize that we aren't the only ones facing a challenge, we're able to get off of the metaphorical soap box and stop feeling like we're all alone. This is very important because there are people out there who think that they have the worst luck in the world and that bad things only happen to them. They will even joke and say that they are cursed and destined for mishaps and tragedy. If that's you... That's not true! You're not the only one who goes through struggles and most importantly, you're not alone! The truth is that we all experience our own versions of difficulties and it is this similarity with others that can create a sense of connection and even empathy towards those around us. This allows for us to talk about our problems and also to talk them out. It reminds us that we are a small part of a whole. We weren't the first ones on earth and we won't be the last. Life, along with its many experiences will continue and go on. Everyone struggles from time to time and some of them may even be struggling right now. Furthermore, someone might even be struggling with what you are currently dealing with. Knowing this grants us the opportunity to relate with them and maybe even work together to find solutions to mutually shared issues. Also, we must also take into consideration the possibility that we might not be the first ones that have dealt with our lemons. There may be hundreds, if not thousands, of people who may have already experienced your current hardship. This allows for two things. For one, you can have hope that if they made it through the trial, you will too. Secondly, you have the option to reach out to them and learn from their experiences and responses. What worked? What didn't? How did they do it? This will provide a unique advantage for you when dealing with your current situation since you will be able to address the challenges or issues with the knowledge, tools, and experience of others as well as your own. It's a recipe for success!

And then there is also the complexity of challenges. There are people around us who may be dealing with some serious issues. When you see your problem in the light of what they are experiencing, your lemon doesn't seem all that important anymore. Losing your job doesn't seem as bad as losing a loved one. A breakup doesn't seem as bad as a terminal illness. Now, I'm not in favor of comparing yourself to others but you have to know that there are people out there who are better off than you but also those that have it worse than you do. When you see things from this perspective, you're able to see that your problem and its solution is not as important as supporting those who are experiencing harder times than you. When you see someone on a hospital bed, you stop focusing on money problems and start appreciating that you're healthy and whole. Quite possibly, you may even temporarily forget about your financial issues and provide some much needed funds for their cause. After all, you are healthy and able to recover those funds with time and effort. They might not. The key to all of this is to see the whole picture. Get the full view. Know that you're not alone when dealing with problems, know that others may be dealing with or have dealt with your current problem, and find out what they did or are doing to overcome it. And lastly, always remember that your problem, no matter how big you think it is, might be minuscule if compared to those of others. Keep things in the proper perspective and you'll see how giant heaps slowly start looking like tiny anthills.

Lemons might be your Opportunity

Have you ever wondered who invented the wheel, crowdfunding, crop rotation, or the artificial heart? I know I have! Yet, more important than knowing who invented them is to focus on the reason for their invention in the first place. You see, most often we tend to focus on the end result, the accomplishment, or the finished product. And that's not a bad thing but when we do so, we can forget about the process or its reason for being or existing. Why is this important? Well, because most great inventions and innovations often started with a lemon. Believe it or not, it's true! **Problems and challenges create the conditions and environment necessary for the development and creation of innovative and breakthrough solutions**. It is this opportunity that makes lemons so important.

Lemons provide opposition along with multiple opportunities and it is necessary for us to see the opportunity "in spite of" the opposition. Notice the use of "in spite of" and not "instead of". This is important because lemons are not meant to be ignored. Ignoring lemons may just as well be ignoring the many opportunities that they may provide. Why would anyone ignore opportunities for self-awareness, development, breakthrough, etc? Well, maybe because they'd rather ignore the challenge or problem than face it, struggle with it, and squeeze the opportunities out of it. When you deal with an issue, you'll see that the solution or solutions are really just opportunities waiting to be released. It is this simple cycle that, over the history of mankind, has fueled the development of millions of tools when dealing with problems or challenges.

Let's revisit the wheel for a moment. The wheel, in its most basic form, was simply the by-product of finding a solution to more efficient transportation. It wasn't like if there weren't means of transportation available but rather that there was an opportunity to find a more efficient and reliable way. People had animals to ride and could walk but they were lacking the means to ease the weight of burdens, transport large objects, and expend less energy. It was these very challenges that brought about the creative thinking process necessary for the development of the wheel. Let's think about this for a minute. What would you have done if you were there? You had a challenge in front of you. All you had was what already existed and what was available to you. You would have several options. You could either ignore the need for more efficient transportation, wait for somebody else to address it, or take on the challenge, struggle with it, and squeeze out the opportunities found therein.

This is of sublime importance because seeing the opportunity in spite of the opposition isn't easy. I mean … It's easy to say it but to actually do it requires effort. It takes getting up close and personal with your problem, knowing it inside and out, and finding the opportunities. It entails the arduous process of analysis, creative thinking, postulation, theory crafting, trial and error, success and failure, investment of time and money, etc. All of this takes a considerable amount of time and effort and it's so much easier to use common solutions to problems or ignore them altogether rather than taking on the challenge and finding the opportunities hidden within. The choice is ultimately ours though. But I highly recommend the latter option.

There will be individuals who experience challenges and look for opportunities. There are others who see a problem and create their own opportunities. Whatever the case may be, there is potential in every challenge. Opportunities can come in the form of personal growth, professional growth, financial gain, relationship building, human advancement, as well as the acquisition of intellectual, moral, spiritual, and/or emotional capital to name a few. Some opportunities may even lead to life-changing epiphanies or world changing inventions and innovations while others just build us up slowly over time.

In life we are constantly investing our time, effort, and energy in making a good life for ourselves, our families, and others. We want to be successful and if we're honest with ourselves, it's a task we must work on daily. Through doing so we are able to build up potential. This potential (energy) can be a catalyst for a better life, better relationships, better experiences, etc.

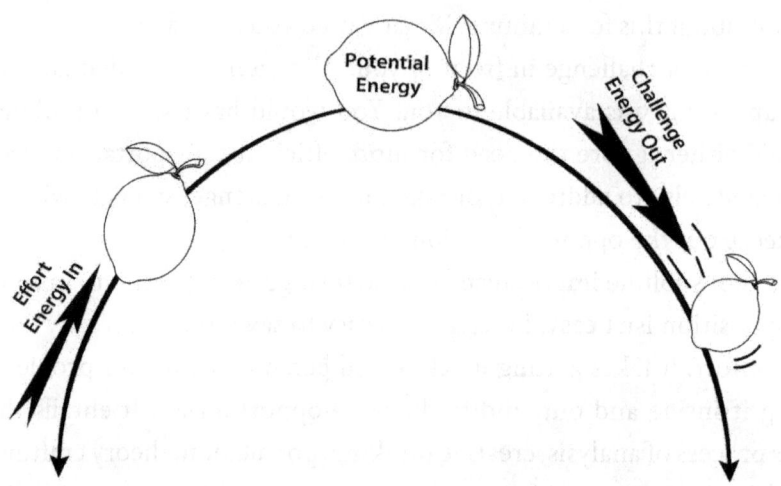

But when lemons come our way, they sometimes tend to make us lose some progress since we have to invest our time and energy in dealing with them. The potential for growth and process is diffused temporarily by the challenge. However, we shouldn't see this as a loss, especially if you focus on the opportunities provided. The fact of the matter is that we sometimes fail to see the whole picture. When you step back and see the experiences as a whole, you notice that even though the challenge did cause you to lose some ground, it actually provided some downward kinetic energy that you can channel upward to get you to the next level. The key is to "use"

the downward pull of the challenge and use the momentum to climb back up to where we were before and beyond.

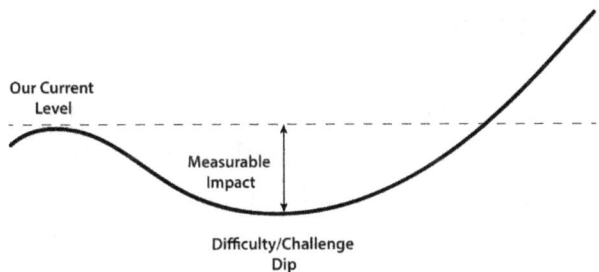

The challenge dip may have a measurable impact on your progress in life, but addressing it and overcoming it means that you're on your way back up. As a bonus, when you step further back and see your life as a whole, you're able to see how all of your lemons were only setups for great growth opportunities. When you compare your long-term growth with growth from a specific challenge, you begin to realize that every challenge was an opportunity to grow and that the culmination of all of the challenges that you've overcome make you who you are today. In general, the ultimate goal when facing a challenge should be to come out better than we were before. Every experience provides small incremental growth opportunities which, in the long-run, equate to significant growth and progress.

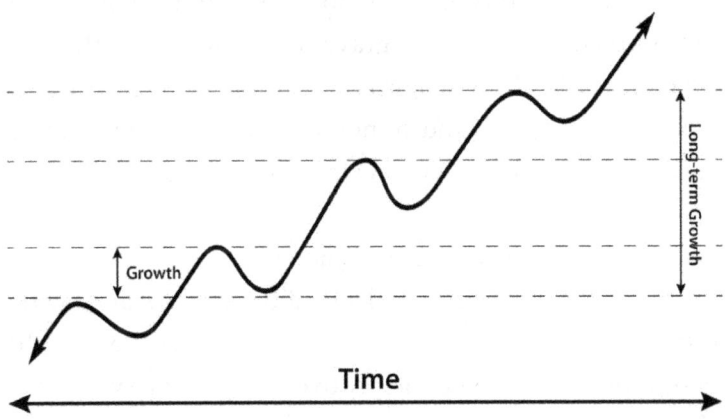

To further illustrate this point, let's liken the problem and opportunity cycle to a journey. A group of individuals are on their way to a new destination. On the road, they realized that a mountain stands before them. There is no clear way across. No detour signs. Just a big fat mountain in the middle of the road. Here is what happens. One person just gives up and sits by the side of the road pouting. Another decides to walk back to where they started and forget about the journey altogether. Another decides to set up camp and wait for the mountain to move or for someone else to find a way around it. Another is convinced that it is simply an illusion and keeps trying to walk through it. Another gets excited, takes out their hiking gear, and starts up the mountain. One even decides to walk around the entire mountain while another gets a pickaxe and starts picking away at the mountain.

Yet there was still one who took several steps back and observed the mountain carefully. After some time, they drew near and took samples of it. After making a few calls and a few deals, they had a contractual agreement to mine half of the mountain. Then, time passed. Everyone that arrived on the other side had their own experience to share. The one who walked around the mountain had strong legs and published a nature book that they created along the way. The hiker shared the new hiking contraption that they had created to make the climb easier. The one who picked his way through the mountain had uber-muscular arms and had even created a rock and gravel company. And, the one with the mining contract held the majority of the shares in a very successful and lucrative rare materials and minerals enterprise. Furthermore, the mining operations had consequently created a path across the ridge of the mountain.

You see, everyone experienced success commensurate to their response to the challenge. Everyone had a different rate of growth based on their response even if they all faced the exact same challenge. Although just an analogy, the basic concepts apply to our experience with challenges as well. There will be those who experience challenges and give up, those who wait for things to change or someone else to do it, and those who take on the challenge head-on. For those who take on the challenge, there will always be a difference in their interaction with the challenge and the end product of their experiences. Always remember, though, that more important than *how successful we are* is the realization that in spite of the challenge we *are indeed successful.* Don't wait until someone else finds the opportunity and don't just use their opportunity. Look for your own opportunity in spite of the opposition and always remember that your success and story can serve as motivation for all those who come behind you. Just like paving the road across the mountain in the journey analogy.

A Proactive Approach to Life's Lemons

Now that we've demystified life's lemons and discovered the hidden potential within them, it is necessary to provide a framework for maximizing our success when dealing with them. The key to a successful encounter with challenges is to be ready and prepared. Readiness creates steadiness and proper preparation prevents poor performance. Being ready for anything and prepared for it allows for us to be proactive and not reactive. Being ready involves knowing that something might happen and being prepared means knowing what to do when it actually happens. Knowledge is power and that power can be exactly what you need to conquer your lemons. A proactive approach when dealing with life's many challenges can be to:

I. Anticipate the challenge.
II. Engage the problem upon arrival.
III. Analyze the problem and get proper perspective.
IV. Implement your action plan.
V. Revise the plan as needed and set up safeguards if necessary.

By following a simple framework like this one, you will have a unique advantage over the challenges you may face. Furthermore, having a strategy can mean all the difference in your success with your lemons.

Anticipate the challenge

It is important that we learn to anticipate and properly identify the subtle nuances of future challenges. These can be apparent and clearly noticeable, or they may be deeply hidden and waiting to sprout up. Whatever it may be, we have the ability to identify patterns in behaviors, relationships, and emotions that may bring about hardships. Additionally, it is possible to identify environmental changes, shifts in cultural climate, and societal changes that can also create problems for us. Knowing this allows for us to be watchful, in a state of continual readiness, so that we don't get blindsided by them. There's nothing worse than being caught off guard or by surprise by something unpleasant. If you don't believe me, ask a 140-pound wide-receiver that just got hammered down by a 380-pound defensive lineman. Ouch! This is an interesting reference because being ready implies being watchful. Not only of our immediate surroundings or of what's in front of us, but also of what is behind us and in the distance all around us. If you can identify it, you can be ready for it.

Engage the problem

One of the most neglected concepts when dealing with challenges is the strategic advantage of engaging them as they arrive. Doing so allows for us to be in control of the situation and to properly keep track of it. It's one thing to anticipate it, but it's another thing entirely to engage and address it. Failure to engage and address problems "now" may cause them to pile up and/or be forgotten. If you piled up all of your lemons to one side, they would eventually rot and cause a stink in your life, not to mention all the bugs they would create. Furthermore, forgetting about a problem doesn't make it go away. It simply gives it ample time to grow and develop until it becomes a real serious issue. Those forgotten and rotten lemons would soon create a lemon tree farm in your life.

I get it! Nobody likes problems and nobody likes solving problems all the time, but ignoring them and pushing them off to the side will only temporarily deter the inevitable issues they will create in your life. The truth is that **it takes more energy to ignore a problem than it does to actually address it.** It doesn't mean that you have to have a solution for it right away, or that you have to have an answer for everything, it just means that you need to be aware of its presence and know what it's about. Don't let your lemons or problems mind their own business, they ARE your business.

Think about it! If you address that relationship problem early on, or that staff member, or that outstanding account, or that pain on your side, you can save yourself from breakup, a rift in your team, delinquency, or a life-threatening infection. And although it may seem like all you do is solve problems, at least they won't pile up on you, surprise you, or get too heavy for you to carry. Trust me, just like a lemon seed, even the smallest issue left unresolved can grow to become a huge problem-causing tree that will take way more energy and resources to fix. So the next time a problem comes your way, just nip it in the bud right then and there and then focus on the important things in life.

Analyze the problem and get the right perspective

Once you engage the challenge, you need to be able to break it down to its integral parts to better understand it and have the right perspective. During this phase, I like to use the COOP strategy as a reminder of what I can do.

COOP

- C - Challenge (What is it specifically?)
- O - Origin (Where does it come from? What is the root cause?)
- O - Opportunities (How can I make it work for my benefit and that of others?)
- P - Perspective (Am I making it bigger than it really is?)

First, you must clearly define the actual challenge. What is actually happening right now? Then, you must figure out the origin of the issue. Where did the problem originate? What is the cause of the issue? Third, you have to ponder on the opportunities that are presented by that challenge. What opportunities can arise for you out of these challenges? How can this situation end with a win for you or for others? Finally, analyze the perspective. How are you viewing the problem? How does it compare to other people's challenges? Do you know anyone who has endured a similar challenge? How did they survive it? Do you remember facing a similar obstacle in life? How did you survive it? This line of questioning provides the information necessary to effectively deal with the challenge.

Think about it! You'll know exactly what the problem is and where it came from. You'll know its root cause and how to prevent it in the future. You'll also discover the hidden opportunities waiting to be revealed, all while maintaining the right perspective. Additionally, you will even have the wisdom and experience with similar encounters by yourself and others as a tool for dealing with the challenge and any future challenges. Not a bad trade-off, right?

Implement your action plan

The knowledge that you acquire through analyzing your problem will serve as a basis for your response to it. Again, you are not reacting to it. You are responding. Not only that, but it is a premeditated response that only fluctuates slightly based on your initial analysis of the situation as it arrives. The goal is to be ready with your action plan beforehand. A great example of this can be insurance policies or emergency funds. Having an insurance policy or an emergency fund is a type of preparation for when accidents happen. If you're in a car wreck or other accident, you can respond to the event with your premeditated action plan. It could be something like this:

STEP 1. Stay calm and make sure everyone is okay and out of immediate danger.
STEP 2. Notify the insurance agency and authorities of the incident as soon as possible.
STEP 3. Verify that all documentation was made and that proof is available of the incident.
STEP 4. Follow up on the claim and make sure it's conducted accurately and that everybody gets what they deserve.

Now, your action plan must be adaptable to the situation. If people are in danger or someone is seriously hurt, you must be able to adapt your response immediately. If you don't have insurance, then adapt your plan. I've found it helpful to have a plan for at least a few variations of any potential challenge. That way, I can respond strategically instead of reacting emotionally and in the moment. I'm not worrying about it, neither am I entertaining the thought that it might happen, but I do make a quick plan in case it ever was to happen to me. Then it's done! Out of my mind and I don't think about it anymore.

Now, we have to stop for a moment and discuss the life cycle of lemons, since it will inevitably affect our planning. In general, when life gives you a lemon, there is tension. The tension may be in the form of physical, financial, spiritual, emotional, social, or any other type of stress. This tension or stress, is the "souring" effect that we feel when engaging a challenge. It is important to note that the stress is only as prolonged as our response-time in addressing the issue at hand.

A Proactive Approach to Life's Lemons

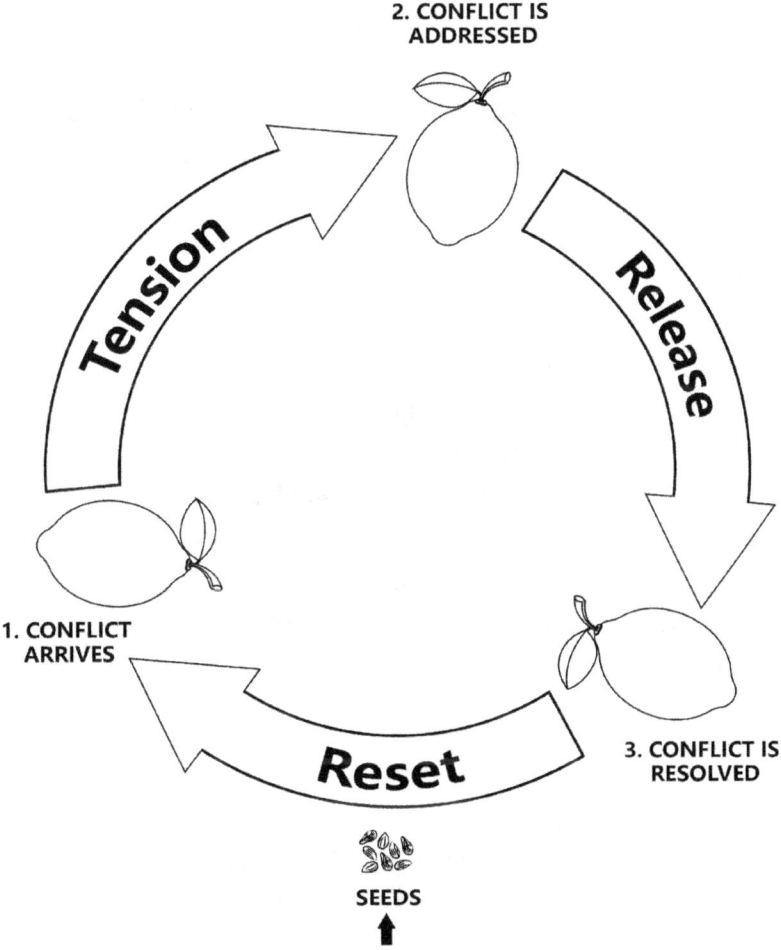

Once it is addressed via our action plan, a release of the pressure, stress, or tension will begin until it is fully resolved and dealt with. However, we must take into account that lemons have a pesky way of reproducing themselves through their seeds. Sometimes we plant the seeds through our lifestyle, sometimes others plant them against our will, and sometimes life just brings them about without warning. Regardless of how they are plated, some issues and challenges will reset themselves and restart either in the same form or in a different form. The good news is that having a flexible plan will definitely help in our continued success with recurring challenges.

Revise the plan and set up safeguards

The most important thing when facing a challenge is to be ready and prepared for it with a flexible plan so that you are proactive and not reactive. Everything else can be modified. Flexibility means that your plan is adaptable and able to change depending on need. Additionally, it may even mean that your plan is versatile and useful in several different scenarios. This works especially well when we encounter truly unique challenges that we couldn't have ever thought up. Using one of our existing action plans, we can make quick modifications on-the-fly and still end up on top of the situation. The plan can be like the linear model shown above. When conflict arrives there will be tension. This is what makes it uncomfortable for us. The tension will remain until the conflict is addressed or ignored. If it is addressed, then there is a sort of release of tension as things start getting back to normal. At this point, you implement the safeguard in order to stop the reproductive cycle. Then, Viola! It will stop or at least be slowed down.

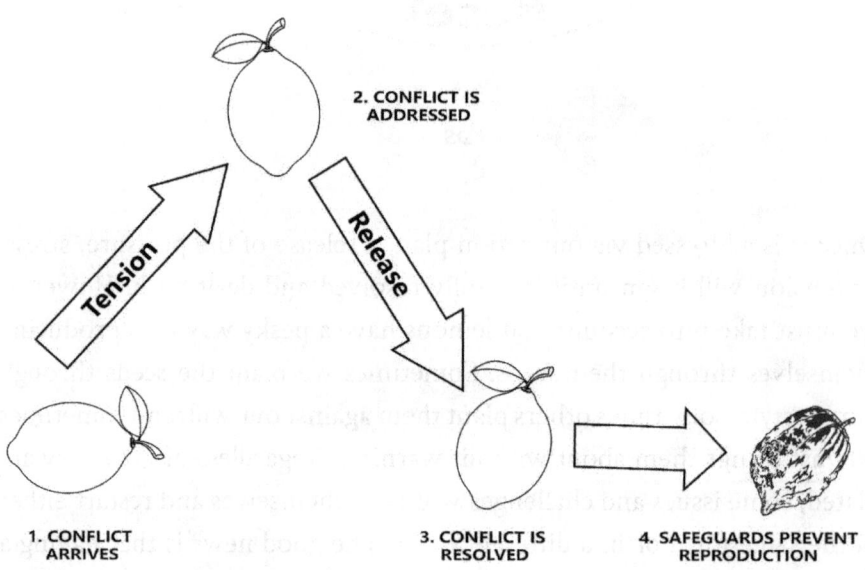

1. CONFLICT ARRIVES
2. CONFLICT IS ADDRESSED
3. CONFLICT IS RESOLVED
4. SAFEGUARDS PREVENT REPRODUCTION

A Proactive Approach to Life's Lemons

Safeguards are implements, either physical, emotional and or spiritual, that we set in place in order to avoid the same problem or minimize the effects of a similar problem in the future. In many cases we are able to use these when dealing with our lemons. You see, we can't enjoy life to the fullest if we are constantly having to deal with issues. Yes, problems are a part of life, but believe it or not, some problems are preventable. And even if they're not, they can still be avoided. Think of it as a guard rail surrounding a tall lookout. The guard rail is in place in order to prevent people from falling off the edge.

In the same way, we are able to set up safeguards in certain areas of our lives where we have struggled in the past or for those that we really don't want to struggle with in the future. For example, if you've had a tough time with relationship problems, maybe you need to analyze your selection of mates, your attitude, etc. Find out where the problem originates, isolate it, and set up some safeguards to mitigate its expression in future relationships. If it is your attitude, then have a daily reminder to "check yourself" in place. If it's a type of personality you attract, know the signs and look for somebody different.

In regard to prevention, safeguards like healthy eating, sleeping, and hygiene habits allow for us to bypass some potential problems that can be brought about by our lifestyle. This is especially helpful when dealing with hereditary issues, behaviors, and lifestyles that you can't control. Think about it. If you know what can happen, why not set up safeguards and try to prevent it from happening. If diabetes or family violence runs in the family, get on a low sugar diet and enroll yourself in some behavior management classes now. Try to set up safeguards that can possibly ensure that the same issues will never happen again. Most times, things can be prevented. If you know something or someone can trigger you and cause you to act in ways that are unnatural to you, remove them from your life. Choose your peace and sanity over winning an argument or debate or always trying to be right. Triggers can show up as people, things, relationships, situations, environments, food, habits, certain practices, and so much more.

If a repetitive situation arises in your life, respond differently. Remember, the definition of insanity is doing the same thing over and over again, but expecting different results. Choose differently! Set up safeguards please. It's really up to us at the end of the day, but I found that it's easier to avoid as many problems as I can instead of having a ton of them pile up on me. That way, I can truly focus on the opportunity in the challenges and not on their quantity.

Balancing Your Lemons

Believe it or not, it is possible to find a way to balance your lemons. You might be wondering why in the world anyone in their right mind would even want them around in the first place. But, remember that we've already established the fact that lemons are unavoidable and that we shouldn't ignore them. So what do we do? We learn to balance them. This is a unique concept and might not be appealing to many but in the real world it is quite useful. The main premise is to acknowledge and learn to appreciate the challenges in order to continually appreciate all of the good breaks and the easy times. All this, while simultaneously making sure that we don't get overwhelmed by challenges but that we still have enough to keep life interesting.

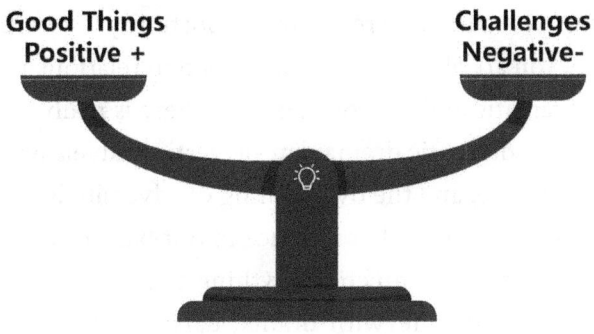

Think of life experiences as a balance beam. If life were too perfect and you had everything you ever wanted, life would be great, right? Well, to a certain extent… yes. But if there wasn't something to strive for, achieve, or overcome it might get dull after some time. It might even get boring. It would lack the opportunity to struggle, achieve, and better yourself. It would lack the risk that makes life so interesting. In addition, when things are only good, we miss out on opportunities to appreciate what we do have. When this happens, we tend to under appreciate people, relationships, possessions, and sometimes even the gift of being alive.

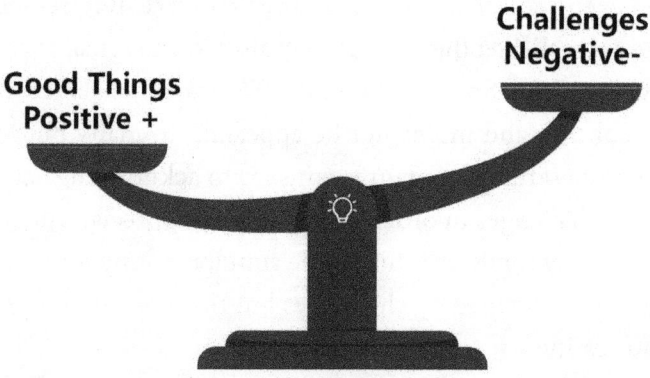

Think about it! We love movies and stories that depict the overcoming of a challenge and a happy ending. But really … would you rather watch a film about the action-packed adventure or the happily ever after? Seriously! Conflict creates plot and plot creates the opportunity to overcome. When you overcome, you are able to appreciate. Even in relationships. Romance is sometimes dramatic and without that risk there is really no enjoyment. I'm not suggesting dramatic drama; I'm suggesting adventurous romance.

Drama, adventure, and the overcoming of adversity is ever present in the human experience and it has its place in our balance beam. However, we must also know that too much of anything can be a bad thing. I mean… try it! Pack your entire life with drama, danger, and dude/damsels in distress and you'll soon wear out your adrenal glands from all of the stress. No thanks! Leave that to the heroes/heroines & secret agents from the movies. If you take on that stress, you will soon find that your life will begin to lack its usual enjoyment.

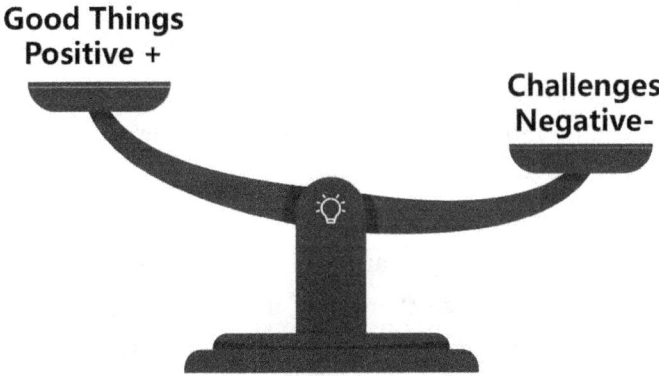

My suggestion is to be smart about the challenges you willingly take on and the extent that you let regular occurrences affect you. Don't shake the lemon tree because those pesky lemons might just fall on your head. But if you have a bucket, pluck them out one by one. They might be useful in the future. Let's face it, a life filled with problems severely inhibits our enjoyment of it. The key to everything is balance and I will even take this a step further, real balance. Most often we think of balance in quantities when we should be thinking about it in quality. That is, balance doesn't mean that if you have five good experiences you need five challenges to appreciate things. It means that the weight of those experiences and their value to you should balance out.

In other words, one problem could be severe enough to throw the scale off and so could a lucky break. Winning the lottery, for example, and receiving a terminal diagnosis will both wreak havoc on your balance beam. But in both scenarios, you would be wise to increase the quality of experiences to balance your life. If you win the lottery, challenge yourself to invest the funds wisely, give to good causes, and create businesses and organizations that will keep you hungry for success and enjoying the adventures that life has to offer.

If you have a terminal illness, do everything that you've ever wanted to do and visit every place you've ever wanted to visit and meet all the people you've ever wanted to meet before you leave this earth. Love, live, and laugh to the fullest. And above all, in both scenarios whether you have a lot of good things or a lot of bad things, give to those around you. That changes everything and brings balance. You see, balance is crucial in experiencing life to the fullest. Don't let the scales tip too much to one side to where you lack enjoyment or too much to the other side to where you lack adventure. Stay balanced! In other words, finding the right balance between good/positive things and tough/negative things is very important in ensuring that you are able to live a full and well life while enjoying and appreciating all that it has to offer. Try not to ever let the bad experiences overwhelm all of the good things that are happening for you. Balance is the key. Whenever you start to feel down about life, make a list of all of the good things that you have and all of the good things that have happened to you. Show appreciation for the things that you have overcome and the accomplishments that you have attained. Then, make a list of all of the bad things that are currently happening or have happened. Analyze your lists. If you notice that you have more good than bad in your life, show gratitude and continue on your course. However, if the bad outweighs the good, you must create an action plan to deal with those negative issues so that you can shape a new, positive life with positive experiences. It may be difficult because it could require making significant changes to your lifestyle and daily habits, but in the end, you will find that it is worth it. While "change" in life is forever present, "balance" in life is crucial.

Once you have created your list of positive and negative life experiences and outcomes, you will be able to create a strategy by pairing them together. For example, having a handicap is seen as a negative thing. On the other hand, if you have been blessed with a special skill or ability that sets you apart from the crowd, this negative situation becomes a positive thing in your life. You may have been born into a low-income family in an economically distressed neighborhood. However, if you become a hard worker and big dreamer who learns to push past life's obstacles to accomplish your goals due to your experiences in life, surely you will be bound to become someone very successful. This is how you pair your negative life experiences with your positive ones to change your outlook on life. When the good times overshadow the bad times, you may lack adventure and opportunity to appreciate the good things in life. Alternatively, if the challenges and negativity begin to outweigh the good times, you may lack enjoyment and excitement about life. Life is all about experiences. You have to learn to be creative in the ways that you approach the different situations that life may bring. Not all of them will be good but they all most certainly will not be bad either. Think about this. Using the list of positives and negatives, see which ones complement each other. See which ones aggravate or diffuse the others. If you lost your job and are unemployed, pair that lemon with what you do have like a skill, talent, craft or unique ability. Who knows, you might even end up starting a business or other venture. Alternately, you may try it the other way. Let's say you are very confident. Well, pair that with a challenge that will test your wits like speaking out for those who are marginalized or even standing up for what is right when no one else does. They are not negative experiences but they are challenges that you willfully can accept to hone your skills and test your metal. Try different combinations between your positive and negative experiences and take a look at how the positive experiences directly, or indirectly, affect and impact the negative ones. Additionally, try to do the opposite. View which challenges overwhelm the positivity that you feel about life. Sometimes, you will notice that your happiness or success is being overcast by draining energies around you. Take note of what these things could be and move with caution. Pay attention to the way others and certain circumstances make you feel about yourself, especially when you were feeling good before they came around. By doing this, you will be able to create a strategy that will not allow negativity to overtake you, but it will also allow you to use the positive experiences in different combinations to complement, mitigate, and/or overcome the lemons of life.

Responses to Life's Lemons

So far, we've discussed several approaches to dealing with life's many challenges. Now, let's take a closer look at what we can do when life gives us lemons. There are four common responses that are available to every single one of us when we encounter challenges, difficulties, and setbacks. Yet, although these are available to us, not all of them are beneficial or preferable. In fact, choosing which one will work best for us depends entirely on our belief system. Let's take a look at them. **When life gives you lemons...don't give up!**

The first thing we need to consider when dealing with problems is that they have the potential to really impact our lives. Although we all face challenges to varying degrees, all of us also have a unique breaking point. That means that a seemingly simple problem for one person can be a catastrophic event for another.

When venturing into this terrain, we must be real while also being empathetic. We must be strong and brave while also being understanding of weaknesses. In addition, challenges can also wear away at even the strongest resolve and will. That means that we are all vulnerable to some degree to become overwhelmed and want to give up. My advice to you is, **never give up!** There would be no need to mention this unless it was really an option. And, it is an option taken by some. Giving up is real and it can take the form of many different things. For one, giving up can mean that you are no longer hopeful that a certain situation will resolve. You are no longer hopeful that a relationship will work out. In response, you let go of any opportunities for future success and dissolve the relationship and/or turn away from the difficult situation entirely. This is a fair and valid response when dealing with challenges, but it is a "defeated" approach. I don't recommend it.

Now, I'm not advocating for self-torture, especially if the circumstance or situation poses significant danger or potential harm to yourself or others. What I'm saying is that if there is a valid reason to keep up the fight, then do so. The benefits of overcoming a situation or resolving a relationship issue may be of great value to you in the long run. For example, some individuals may have been involved in severe conflict with a family member or close friend and then decide to cut them out of their lives indefinitely.

Now, again, there are many valid reasons for disassociating yourself from those that don't have your best interest in mind, but we also have to analyze our decision and see if our choice was really the right choice or just a "I don't want to deal with this anymore" strategy. Another example can be as simple as this. I've known people that give up on a career simply because they encounter several challenges. Others give up on a business or an idea simply because the initial challenges and investment outweigh the immediate benefits. Yet, what if all we had to do was stick with it and push on? What if the best relationship we've ever had could be born out of initial disagreement? What if the next million dollar idea was incubating in that business you gave up on or that career path that you left behind?

Then, there are also those who give up on life altogether when the challenges get too tough. Some people actually resign themselves to any hint of prosperity, positivity, and progression. They give up on life and live mundane and meaningless lives. I don't mean to be harsh, but this is true. They just go through the motions and survive. This can happen to any one of us. It's happened to me. It is a serious state where you just can't seem to see ahead. You're lost. You go through life just existing with no hopes, dreams, or aspirations. Just like a zombie. Those lemons become so oppressive that they cause us to lose sight of anything else. If you've ever found yourself in this place or you're there right now, take courage!

Life is so much more than what we lost or what we don't have anymore. Things might never be the way that they used to be. We might never be able to hold that loved one again. We might not be able to do what we used to do but we must always remember that it's not over. There is still so much more to experience. And this is also true for those of us who have contemplated ending life because of the pressure of challenges. Don't listen to those lemons and their voices no matter how loud they may get. Trust me! I know what it's like. But I also know that it's not true. It's not over! You're not done! There's so much more! If you can still breathe then there's still room to experience life. The pain is only temporary and a reminder that we are still living. My advice is to **push forward, take courage, and never ever give up**. Find at least one thing that brings you fulfillment and joy and grab onto that. Reach out to those that can help you. Don't suffer alone! You don't have to! Create a network of support and then build up strength until you're finally able to take on those pesky lemons on your own. Even then, you won't be alone. You have everyone who loves you on your corner.

When life gives you lemons, make lemonade!

This age-old adage is the one that inspired the writing of this book. For many many years, that's exactly what I would do and recommend to others. Just roll with the punches and get your workout in. Honestly, this is a perfectly reasonable and viable strategy when dealing with life's lemons. When they arrive in your life, you take them and beat the juice out of them, to put it nicely. You see, making lemonade is a great way to approach lemons because you don't ignore them. You address a challenge and squeeze the potential out of it and this is a good thing. Yet, I've come to realize that this approach is very ego-centric and ultimately only benefits ourselves. It's also a type of "make the best of it" mentality.

When we make lemonade, we are technically coping with a problem instead of looking for solutions. Once the issue resolves, we simply discard the problem just like we do with the lemon peel, pulp, and seeds after we've squeezed the juice out. When you make a glass of lemonade, who drinks it? Who enjoys it? For how long do you enjoy it? I know this is analogous but think of it in terms of a real life challenge. If you don't have a job, you got yourself a problem right? That's your lemon. Instead of ignoring your problem or giving up and living on the streets, you decide to take on the challenge, better yourself, and look for a job. In doing so you're making lemonade. You'll drink that metaphorical lemonade until you finally get your job. You're making the best of the situation. This is good and very useful in our life journey. Yet, there are still other alternatives to consider.

When life gives you lemons, start a lemonade stand!

Is it just me or does a lemonade stand always remind you of a kid behind a cardboard stand selling a cold glass of lemonade for a couple of cents? At first thought, this might seem like a childish and silly approach but upon closer examination, we can see how doing so might bring even more value out of those pesky lemons that we experience from time to time. Lemonade stands have one purpose in mind and that is to sell a product. In our case, it's lemonade. In comparison to the "make lemonade" approach, the lemonade stand approach differs in that the lemonade is not just meant to be consumed by its maker to pass the time but also used as a way to gain profit. Profit is a main focus here. Profit by definition is what you get after you subtract costs from your sales and income. In a "give up" approach, you lose money. In a "make lemonade" approach, you break even. But, in a "lemonade stand" approach, you make a profit! This is a small business mentality that aims at not only overcoming a challenge but also creatively looking for opportunities hidden within the lemons. Additionally, it's a great way to serve and benefit those around you. All of this while staying productive during a challenge and staying ahead of the competition.

Let's use the same scenario as before. Not having a job is the challenge. Then, not giving up and finding a job is making lemonade. Realizing that others are unemployed as well, creating a resume writing service to help them, and creating a second source of income while finding a new job simultaneously is starting a lemonade stand. In this approach, you not only solve the initial problem but you squeeze out the potential and opportunity to do even greater things. Opportunity varies widely but inside of every lemon there's bound to be at least one possibility to make profit.

Personally, I started my lemonade stand when I became unemployable due to a disability. For a year and a half I wasn't able to work or pretty much do anything. Well, at least not able to work traditionally. While facing this unique lemon, I looked deep within and discovered that although I couldn't work the way that I used to and in the field that I preferred, I could still work in my own capacity. I began selling books and textbooks online at first, then I focused on surplus sales. Eventually I got into imports and exports. But it didn't stop there, I continued to serve those around me, show them the process of online sales, and even donated hundreds of items to help others start their business or support their organizations. Yet, as mentioned before, I wanted to return to the field of education. You see, the lemonade stand approach wasn't an alternative to what I wanted to do, it was in addition to what I wanted to do. Complementarian, if you will. As you know, I eventually returned to the traditional workplace but maintained the side hustle until I eventually passed it on to someone else. Now, I'm certain that there are thousands if not millions of lemonade stand stories out there and I'd encourage everyone to make theirs. It is these stories of success and opportunity in the face of obstacles that enrich the human motivational arena. However, we can't help to ask the question, what happens to a lemonade stand when the lemons run out? As mentioned before, lemons come in varying degrees of impact and quantities. There may be seasons filled with them and others where they're completely absent in our lives. So how do you continually squeeze the potential out of lemons?

When life gives you lemons...start a lemon product enterprise!

This approach aims at expanding on the original lemonade stand approach when dealing with challenges. Taking the small business concept a step further allows for us to maximize on the opportunities provided in the entire lemon, not just the juice. More often than not, we use the lemons for their juice and nothing more. Yet, there is still much more available for use inside. When relating it to a challenge or problem, it can mean finding a way to squeeze potential out of it and in its entirety and not just in one way. In a lemon products enterprise approach, we're able to metaphorically squeeze the lemon to create our lemonade product for mass consumption as an immediate goal. We can then use the rind and pulp to create lemon-scented and flavored products and garnishes as a short-term goal. And, we can also plant the lemon seeds as a long-term goal. It may sound ludicrous, but it is actually possible to use a challenge for long term success.

For further insight, let's revisit the life cycle of problems/challenges. We know that when conflict arrives, it produces tension and discomfort. We also know that when we address the problem we trigger the release phase. And finally, we know that once the problem is resolved or the challenge is overcome there is potential for the lemon to reproduce itself. Well, in the enterprise approach, you accept it as it is. But, you don't view it cyclically. You view it as an upward spiral because you're not just solving a problem or overcoming a challenge, you are actually setting up a system for continual success with the problem that produces your desired outcomes.

With every success, you are able to squeeze more and more potential out of your lemon and increase your knowledge, ability, expertise, etc. When we plant the lemon seeds strategically, we are in control of the reproductive process. And, that's a good thing!

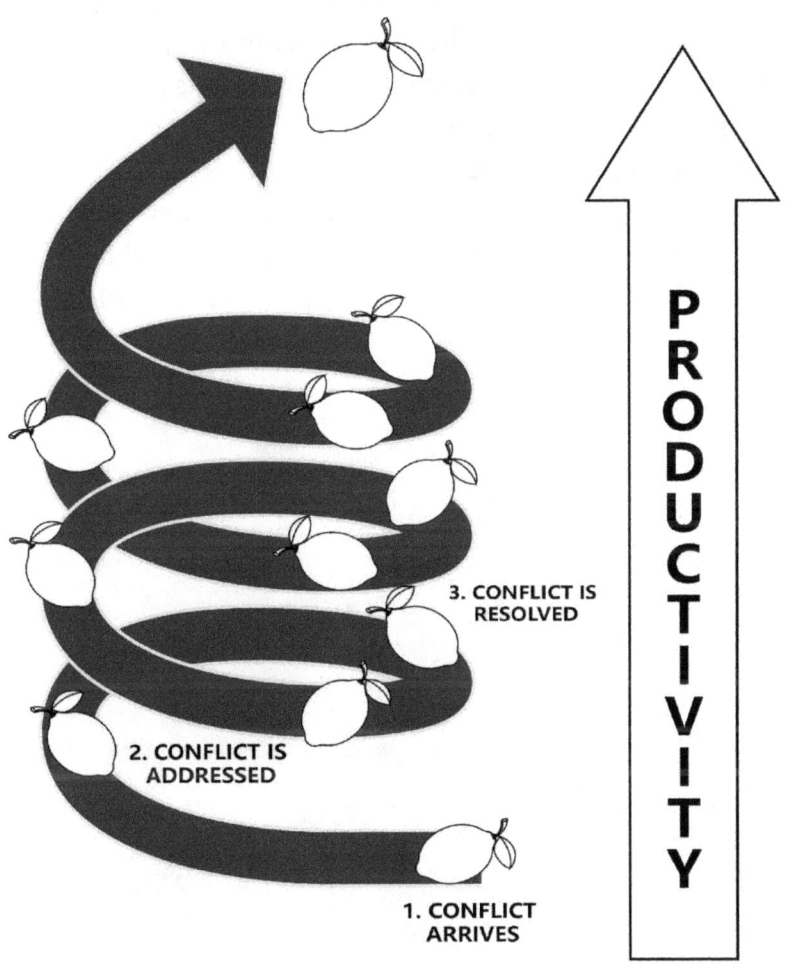

The question that we should really be asking is, why would anybody want to keep the problem around indefinitely? The answer to it is simple. It's not about you it's about others. If we can continue to help others through the challenge, then we should. Additionally, there are some challenges that cannot be resolved quickly, not even with time and effort. Some challenges are long term. Whenever you start an enterprise when faced with a long-term challenge, you engage it completely and skillfully extract all of its potential. This experience is what we must focus on because it can be shared with others who may be facing or are facing your challenge. This approach is unique in that it is primarily a way to help others and to continually crush a type of lemon until its secrets are fully revealed to the world. These secrets can be key to other people's successes with it. So, instead of giving up, rolling with the punches, or solving your problem by helping others, you're focusing fully on creating a systematic approach for others to use so that they can create their own small businesses. You become the provider for them. It's the equivalent of creating a franchise system.

The Lemon's Product Enterprise System

In order to understand this concept more fully, let's break it down to its individual components. The word enterprise is defined as a business or company and also a project that is difficult and requires effort. This forms the basis for the concept. It is a venture with profit as a goal that will require effort. On the other hand, we have the word system. A system is defined as a set of things working together as part of a whole and also a set of procedures and principles according to how something is done. In other words, it is a set of concepts that collaborate to create a procedural method. Merge both words and we can summarize that **an enterprise system is the unique way in which a multi-faceted process is implemented to engage a challenge and produce maximum profit.** It is the challenge and its respective opportunity to make profit that spurred this book to life. We've already established that we will all face challenges and that they may present new opportunities for us. We've also discussed the options that we have when engaging these and how we can remain productive through the experiences. Now, we will discuss the systematic and strategic approach to fully taking advantage of the challenges and capitalizing on the opportunity. An enterprise system is a big business mentality with long-term sustainability as a core goal. It entails creating multiple streams and lifelines in order for the company to reap benefits from different sources at different times. Also, it is systematic which means that it is planned, strategic, synergetic, and efficient and of course somewhat automated. This is important because the goal is not to continually focus all of your effort on the problems and opportunities but to establish the methodology necessary to create an automated system that will work on its own and provide you the benefits in the long run. That is not to say that you will not have to fine-tune it and check up on it from time to time but as long as the system is running, you can instead focus mostly on the opportunities, growth, and profits and, of course, new opportunities. How is this applicable? Well, when we face a challenge or life gives us those lemons, we can use this framework and thought process to:

I. Identify the challenge.
II. Dissect it to its integral parts.
III. Identify global and specific opportunities found in the challenge.
IV. Create a process to not only act on the opportunities but also to sustain and grow them.
V. Receive the profit gained in whatever form that may come and use the capital to benefit those around us, those who are facing the same challenge, and the world at large.

Identify the challenge

Knowledge is power and power can mean the difference between winning or losing. When the challenge presents itself, be ready to identify it. Don't let it be like that tree or fruit that you ignore or miss in your garden. Don't generalize and say that everything is wrong. Focus in. Use the process of elimination and find the patterns to isolate the main issue. Once you do so, you will be able to get a closer look into its inner workings.

Dissect the challenge

Problems and challenges are not as basic as we may think. Although some might be simple and straightforward, some may be very complex. If we are to fully understand the inner workings of the problem in order to cancel its negative effects and find the hidden opportunities, we must break the problem down to its integral components and parts. This is where who, what, when, where, why, and how come into play. Ask the questions. Dive deep into the issue and the reason behind each individual component and you will see that the solution to the problem might be different than what you had expected.

Identify global and specific opportunities

Exposing the inner workings of the challenge allows for us to see how each component works in synchrony to make up the challenge in its entirety and original form. This allows for us not only to identify any global opportunities such as those presented by the general challenge, but also the individual opportunities that can be found in specific components within the challenge itself.

Create an action and sustainability plan for the opportunities

Once you dissect the problem and find the many opportunities within, you may begin the process of choosing which opportunities you will focus on. A good practice is to categorize the opportunities by level of impact, resource requirement, and longevity. Doing this will allow for you to use your time and effort wisely and get a bigger bang for your buck, so to speak. Then, you can create the actual plan. You can do this in many ways but I recommend using the SMART goal approach. In it, you verify that the plan is specific, measurable, attainable, reasonable, and timely. This will further refine your strategy and will provide better and more consistent results. Finally, we need to plan for the sustainability of those opportunities that can provide long-term benefits. These can be easily integrated into our lifestyles, rituals, routines, and daily life in order for us to continue to glean the benefits for as long as they are profitable for us.

Reap the rewards and make a difference

As you begin to take action on the opportunities provided by your lemons, you will begin to see results. These may be immediate or gradual. They can be material or immaterial. They may be in the form of money, physical attributes, and tangible resources but may also be in the form of relationships, spirituality, self-discovery, and socio-emotional intelligence. There are many ways that the dividends may be provided to us. However, we must always remember one thing. It's not all about us or for us. I mean, it can if you want to but remember that that's exactly what made "making lemonade" with your lemons and drinking it on your own a "make the best of it" mentality. It's kind of a selfish mentality as well. But that's really up to us. You see, after you have exponentially reaped benefits from your challenge you have the option and maybe even the responsibility to share what you have learned and received with others. It is at this stage that we transcend from **making it** to **making a difference**, we go from **me** to **we**, we go from **surviving** to **leaving a legacy**, from **my story** to **history**.

Example of the Enterprise System

An example of this process can be losing a job because of cutbacks. Identifying the general problem is easy. You lost your job because of budget cuts and have no income. Those are the main issues. However, breaking it down into its integral parts may highlight that the job was cut because the company wasn't producing enough and that you have no income because you depend on a single source. Furthermore, upon closer examination, you realize that you should have seen it coming.

The organization was on the decline and you had the option to boost productivity or to start looking for other employment. The *immediate opportunity* presented by the challenge is the provision of a fresh start with a more productive organization and the prospect of meeting new people, learning new things, and possibly receiving better benefits and compensation. An *individual opportunity* provided can be finding a way to have multiple streams of income through return on investments, hobbies, and side hustles so that you never end up without income again. Another *individual opportunity* can be that of adopting a more vigilant attitude towards work especially in regard to the organization's financial stability. A hidden opportunity would be answering the question, what was my part in the success and/or failure of my employer? What is my work ethic and how does it affect my employment? Could I have done anything different to increase productivity and sales to keep the business afloat? The list may go on and on and if you take the time to think about it you may find some very valuable insight for your benefit. Finally, once the opportunities have been identified it is time to create the processes that will allow for us to capitalize on those opportunities. It works best if we create a process for each opportunity. For example, the process for "skill level development" can be to start reading at least one book a month pertaining to your field of work. This would be a well-structured long-term process. The process for "income flow increase" can be to identify the talents and hobbies you have and see if you can use them to freelance on the evenings, weekends, and holidays to get some extra funds coming in. Then you can invest them back into your freelancing or you can place them in other investments that can provide returns and dividends. This will be a flexible long-term process. Also, a process for "finding a new job" would be to do your research on the organization first. Don't just jump into the next sinking ship unless you intend to keep it afloat. If stability is your goal, then find an established organization whose values you believe in. If quick returns are your preference, then take the chance and then invest the resources you receive and don't waste them. This can be a short term goal that can eventually become a long-term relationship with an organization. Finally, work hard and look for the benefits. These will come in different forms. For one, you may find that due to your diligence and study you may have become an expert in your field. You may also find that the new organization you chose to work for is more aligned to your personal vision and mission than the previous. And what about the new relationships you would have built during that time through your work, investments, and freelancing? What about that new network of resourceful and successful individuals? You may even find that your entrepreneurial freelance venture turned out to be a huge success to the point where you no longer rely on your job as your primary source of income. Yet, it doesn't stop there. The main goal for all of this is the opportunity to share the wealth with those around you. I'm not suggesting that you "make it rain", I am simply saying that you will have the option for philanthropy and "giveft-ing". Giveft-ing, Gifting + Giving, is a word I use to describe giving without expecting anything in return. Just like if it was a gift. Except that you don't need a special occasion. You just give just like if it was a gift. No strings attached. The great news is that you can do this with physical wealth but I am also referring to the wealth of knowledge that you can share with others who are facing or will face your same challenge. Trust me. You are not the only one who has lost their job. It is in sharing our experiences, failures, and success that we get to experience the greatest part of the enterprise system, it's main purpose. We should never forget that every business is dependent on a need from its customers and consumers whether real or perceived. We can never forget that fulfilling the needs around us will keep our enterprise going and expand our network and net worth.

The Anatomy of Lemons

Lastly, I'd like to share some insight that may be helpful in better understanding the Enterprise Approach to Life's Lemons. One of the most common scientific names for the lemons we know is Citrus Limon. It is a species of small, evergreen trees native to South Asia. It can be found flourishing and harvested in many parts of the world today. This is important because life's lemons are not always native to us. Sometimes we plant them ourselves as we said before but most times they just end up in our garden uninvited. Regardless of their origin, they are present. But have you ever wondered what they're composed of? What is a lemon? What is inside a lemon? I know I have. Well, it is said that a lemon is a hybrid of bitter orange and citron. In short, it was naturally selected to be bitter and tart. Yet, we all know that. But what makes it bitter and tart we don't. The answer is... primarily citric acid! Citric acid is a weak organic acid that triggers a sour response for our taste buds but is also essential for the metabolic processes of almost all living things. Acid might burn but it can also benefit living organisms. Have you ever heard the saying "no pain no gain"? What about "if it is good for you, it probably doesn't taste like candy"? Well, that's exactly how lemons are. Exercise is good for us but it can also be painful. Vegetables are great for our bodies and yet chocolate-dipped ice cream tastes so much better right? You see citric acid has many functions. For one, as mentioned above, it is essential for aerobic metabolism. It is also a good preservative and flavor enhancer.

The Lemons of Life

If we focus on the sour factor alone, we can lose sight of the potential benefits that lemons can provide.

Another thing that makes up lemons are its physical characteristics. For one, they are yellow and have a soft but thick exterior shell often called the rind. The yellowish color is derived by the flavonoids contained within, one of them being keratin, which is also very good for our bodies. The rind is composed of two parts. The yellow part we call the zest and the white, soft part we know as the endocarp. Inside the rind we find a series of symmetrical sections known as carpals that contain juice-filled sacs that we call the pulp. There are also seeds that are randomly strewn about on the inside.

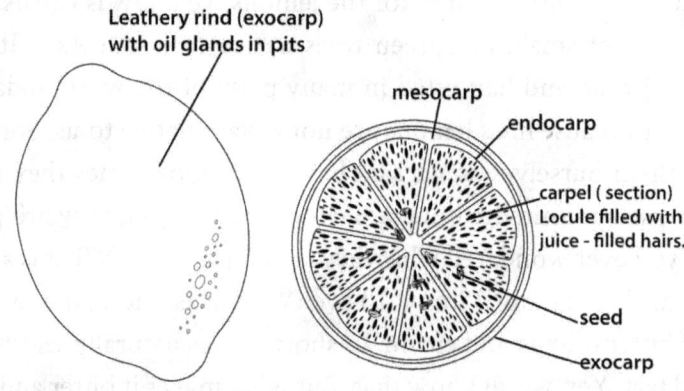

**Hesperidium (berry with a leathery rind)
e.g. lemon (Citrus lemon)**

Each component of the lemon works synergistically to give us a uniquely identifiable fruit. However, each component just like with the challenges we face, also provides an opportunity. For further insight, let's use the analogy of a physical lemon products enterprise.

As soon as the lemons have been picked from your garden, they make their way to your processing plant. The first step in the process would be to accept the lemons as they come. This is the *intake process*. It entails the conscious process of receiving the lemons as life provides them and not ignoring them. In short, you must make space for them. Next, you'll have to sort through them to identify where they come from and if there are any variations. In this step, you'll find the origin of the challenge and also its potency and concentration. Some challenges are single occurrences while some are a compilation or combination of many different issues. To make it more interesting. Sometimes some other fruit gets thrown in the mix with our lemons. These are misinterpretations and misperceptions that we can sort through in this phase. Not everything is a problem or challenge just because it's hard. We need to categorize difficulties accordingly. Not everything is a lemon. Separate the grapefruits and oranges from the lemons and carry on. After you sort through and identify your lemons, you may then begin the process of dissecting them to reveal their individual components. In this "assembly-line" type of approach, you are able to identify specific characteristics and opportunities hidden in specific facets of your challenge. At this stage in the enterprise system, you cut the lemon up and start separating the zest from the rind, the juice, and seeds from the pulp, etc. In doing so, you identify the specific issues found hidden in the challenge. Once they're identified, you can create a plan for each to give you a profit. Okay, so now let's talk about the potential inside of each part of the lemon that you separated. For one, let's use the lemon juice to make lemonade, if you have sugar and water, or just to sell the lemon juice as is. This can be considered an immediate goal and you will be able to immediately capitalize on the opportunity presented by a challenge. However, we shouldn't just stop there. As a short-term goal, you can dry up the zest and add some pepper, if you have any, and start selling your very own condiment and spice product. You can also use the rind and pulp to create soaps, scented candles, and supplements as a mid-term goal and then plant the seeds in your garden as a long-term strategy to grow more lemon trees. Wait a minute! More lemons? Yes! That's the entire point of the enterprise system and it's what makes it different from regular "small business" lemonade stands. **The Enterprise Approach is the systematic and sustainable approach to continually making profit out of a challenge.** But why would you want more of the same problem?

Well, remember that if you have a system in place, it won't really bother you that much anymore, and always remember that for some of us, lemons are not just a one-time thing. Some of us have permanent and long-term challenges to overcome like illness, emotional trauma, losses in physical and cognitive ability and mobility, etc. It is not like we want to keep getting these lemons, it is just that they are and might be there indefinitely. It is this thinking that inspired me to think about the benefits of not only overcoming obstacles and challenges but also getting something out of them long term. It is the "I am still going to finish on top" mentality and it can help many people. I'd like to ask you something. Have you ever seen a paraplegic athlete contending for Paralympic titles and medals? Have you ever seen or met the many emotionally, mentally, and physically bruised and battered service members that succeed at returning to normal life in society as we know it? Have you ever seen cancer survivors' lifestyles? They are all unique and powerfully motivating experiences. Not every challenge is temporary and not every problem can be fixed. The truth is that some will require a lifetime of caution, discipline, and proactive-ness. However, even if you aren't facing any long-term challenges you may still use the enterprise system in a very unique way. Remember that the main goal of the system is to provide a product and/or service to consumers. Well, what if you could provide that product or service continually by using your current challenge and creating a system or process to help others when they go through the same challenge? Instead of wasting the opportunity, you can create a sustainable cycle of reciprocity knowing that someone else at some other point in history will face the same or a similar problem. Let's be honest, maybe the return on investment won't be monetary, although it can be if you market and sell your process, but I am sure that the emotional, charitable, and physiological dividends of helping others will be more than sufficient payment for your trouble... no pun intended! At the end of the day, it would be great to say that you didn't only overcome your lemon but that you set up a system to crush them to pulp daily. And that can be very satisfying.

The Anatomy of Lemons

Going back to planting lemon seeds, it is in this phase that we can control the lemon tree growth, its location in our garden, and the timing for fruit-bearing. This allows for us to develop a sort of resilience and toughness to get us through other challenges that might be different than those we are currently harvesting. Taking control of the challenge will mean that it won't get the chance to control you. You see, if you have control over the lemons and your response to them, you will really be able to see the opportunities in spite of the opposition and capitalize on them for your benefit, and of course, that of others through the use of the Enterprise System Approach. I have counseled many people who feel hopeless, have extended myself to support and create groups/organizations that produce more impact, and have continually replicated myself in the field of education. The great thing is that you can experience success with your lemons and make significant contributions to the world as well. If you already are, then kudos to you! Stay on it and keep on giving. Everything is worth it! We only have one life to live and at a minimum, we get to choose how we use it to leave our mark, no matter how small, on the world.

Conclusion

In closing, it is very important that you keep in mind that lemons are not all that we receive in this life. Just look around you. There is so much to be thankful for and so many opportunities waiting to be seen in the midst of opposition. Lemons are only temporary too, so try not to hold on to them. Lemons should also be kept in perspective. Take a step back, view the bigger picture, and count your blessings because it could always be worse. Always see the opportunity in spite of the opposition because it could be your breakthrough. Regardless of what you are facing, know that I believe in you. I believe in your ability to conquer your lemons of life. I believe in your success regardless of what life may throw your way. When you encounter people going through things that are similar to challenges that you have already faced and conquered, you have the opportunity to relate to them, help them, and encourage them. Living on the streets of Mexico, I saw many individuals enduring financial hardships. I have seen people without any money at all take something as simple as a seashell, capitalize on it by adding string and selling seashell bracelets to make a profit. In their greatest hour of weakness and what seemed like a hopeless situation, they were able to use their creativity to turn their lemons into an entire lemon enterprise. They did not limit themselves to just selling seashell bracelets to locals by the seashore. They went on to sell their bracelets in larger venues and, by expanding their potential, they eventually were able to sell their products in bulk and export them to North America and other countries. They were able to accomplish so much because they viewed the opposition as an opportunity to achieve something great. Some people experience life-long hardships. When you lose a loved one, it is a one-time event that is devastating for a considerable amount of time and we can never truly replace what was lost. Losing a limb or a progressive illness is something that lasts for a lifetime. Both are lemons. Both can provide hidden opportunities if we take the time to look past the disillusionment and grief. While adjusting to new realities, consider how you can use the challenge to benefit others. If you received a lemon like the one mentioned, you could use it to create the next innovative prosthetic limb. In creating it for yourself, you could stumble upon a system of resources that can help a plethora of amputees globally. Other people will be able to see you conquering your lemons and draw inspiration from your courage. Losing a loved one, although painfully difficult, may still provide a venue for you to create and provide counseling and support services. Suffering from progressive illness may facilitate the creation of organizations for mutual-support and the investment in finding a cure or remedy. Whatever your lemons may be, don't waste the opportunity. In my case, I could have stubbornly struggled to remain in the classroom setting thereby influencing thirty students per year, even though I was struggling with severe PTSD and Anxiety. Instead, I chose to let go, accept the challenge, and crush my lemons. Now, I am able to teach others what I know and love about leadership, education, STEM, and enrichment and through them am able to physically serve thousands of students, parents, and staff members annually and many more online. Additionally, I am able to provide free programs and resources for science, technology, engineering, arts, and mathematics (STEAM), and I'm able to make an even bigger impact than I would by just being in the classroom and teaching. If someone experiences domestic violence in their relationship, once they get out of that relationship, they are able to help others around the world who may have previously experienced the same situation. Moreover, they are definitely able to provide aid and resources to those who are currently facing the same difficult situation. Rather than leaving the memory and the lesson of the abuse in the past once it is over, consider starting a movement that works to protect individuals against domestic violence. By doing so, they are able to take the problem that they faced and transform it into a large organization to help people. One thing that you must realize is that there are hundreds and thousands of people who are enduring the same challenges that you are experiencing. You must see other people conquering their lemons and be inspired. Be encouraged. Know that there is nothing that you cannot accomplish once you remove the blinders of self-doubt from your mind and vision. Use your lemons to bless the world around you and do not stop until you have developed the solution that could be the future of something big. You could even start a movement so that individuals who haven't faced specific challenges are able to empathize with others and understand how different things affect people. Furthermore, you can start a campaign and get a legislature passed that ensures the exposure of the problems that you have encountered along with the solutions. The possibilities are endless and you are limitless. I was the child who lived in the lowest and most economically distressed neighborhoods. I lived in Salvation Army locations and transitional living centers. Government housing. On welfare. An absent father. Experience countless physical and emotional abuse. Dropped out of high school as a freshman, and I lived on the streets in Mexico. If I was able to bounce back from all of those lemons and transform my life into something that can help others and encourage them... you can do so much more! I get the privilege to observe the problems that other people are facing and immediately present viable solutions to them. If I am unable to share a solution or method that I have already developed, I do not rest until I am able to provide them with a sense of direction and encouragement. I make it my responsibility to assist every single individual that comes my way with their lemons on their life journey. You only live once. Why not use this life to make a difference? One time someone asked me about mortality. You can become immortalized by touching someone's heart. The religious, political, and inspirational leaders that we know and love are immortalized because of the huge impacts that they made while they walked this earth. Think about the ways that you can make an impact. You

Conclusion

do not have to live a bland life. Remember that lemons are only temporary and troubles do not last forever. Use your lemons to add zest to your life so that you can make a difference and leave your mark!

www.ingramcontent.com/pod-product-compliance
Lightning Source LLC
Chambersburg PA
CBHW060353050426
42449CB00011B/2957